DISTANT

Quarantine Collection vol. 2

Akeem Olaj

Edited by Tova Charles and Chibbi Orduña

DEDICATION

To everyone that took these years of social distancing as a
time to reflect and decide what kind of people are best for
our lives. To letting go of relationships that do not serve
your purpose of healing. To realizing your worth and
charging double for it. Next time Charge Triple...you're
worth it. To knowing what this breathe means to you, to
seeing through the veil of racism and choosing freedom.

so ·cial dis ·tance

noun

1. the perceived or desired degree of
    remoteness between a member of one social
    group and the members of another, as
    evidenced in the level of intimacy tolerated
    between them.

Contents

Flood

During the Covid pandemic
I am forced to sit with myself.
Forced
To let the flood of memories travel to the last
time I was forced to be this still
I tried to make it a fairy tale in 6 parts:

I.
There's a story I use to tell myself about a flood.

How the sky opened up;
How the streets turned to a stream, then
to a river, then
                    to a lake
How the innards of our home went from
Life,
          living room and kitchen,   to empty
          fish tank-now graveyard-algae filled
          aquarium.
          How we humans thought we could push
nature back
          told it not to cross the lines or levy's we
put in place
Nature laughs; then decided it wanted to reclaim
space that was once there's.

II.
There's a story of how we ran.

          Noticed how the city looked... different when
                    driving on the opposite of the highway.
                              We packed "light".
     Two weeks' worth of outfits (mix and matched).
               Calmed nerves by cracking jokes

About how storms have been over exaggerated
Handled with extreme fear
This time was different.

III.
The actual story.

It's 2005, I'm a freshman in college 140 miles
away from New Orleans

The scene: me locked in a condemned dorm room
reopened for college students attending UL
Lafayette
Huddled around the news as they just confirmed
that a seawall caused by this hurricane will
engulf the place I call home.

My mom calls to let me know they have arrived
in Baton Rouge to my cousin's house the day
before.

3 people to a bedroom. 9 people
to 2 bathrooms, eyes: Glued
to the news
the picture: an image of a mini family reunion.
Filled with laughs. Powered
            by the 50 plus years of the meteorologist
claiming that   "This was the big one"

How we all thought we would be home
Soon. How we all thought about the longer school
year to make up for this "extra" time off.

IV
A story of how we were arrogant.

Picture: A New Orleanian buck-jumps[1] to false
alarms for decades. Now, legs magically become
concreate, like an empty foundation of a home
minus a house.

Caught thinking an evacuation was a vacation
instead of our exodus.
Believed; the governments would save those that
couldn't afford to leave on the second day, the
fourth day at the latest, not
the 17th. And then the Story of the flood become
me

And no one laughed the same
afterwards, no smile when street corners signs
became buoys. No joy in a home
becoming abandoned structure washed off
its foundation into the middle
of the street

V
Landmarks now dystopian zones
testing the limits of humanity

Pictures became water stained and erased.

Birth certificates faded and mildewed.

Heirlooms lost in salt and silt and vanished.

Can you still say you survived a flood...if you
evacuated in time? If only your possessions were
submerged in water for days instead of your
body?

1.   Buck jump: a New Orleans Dance Done During A Second
     Line.

3

Will the end result be the same: a complete wash
Wash your skin, wash whatever you could
salvage, rebuild or
pick up your heart that's at the pit of your
stomach or start over somewhere else

Can time truly heal the wounds caused by
disaster capitalism even after it turns profit?
(*Exploiting black flood lines on an abandoned
house for tours*)
Will the culture survive
the overhauled of our school systems?
our integrity?
our way of life?

What no one mentions:
When you leave home after a disaster, People
that didn't, will look at you and
think that you have
everything.

But I still have nothing to show for my
memories. Just hearsay of what I can remember.
Still don't have pictures of my parents when they
were children, nothing in hand
to compare how far my face fell
from the family tree.

No family home in the 9th ward because
when the rain fell and the
levels broke; The foundation of family became a
tombstone.

VI
A memory without a eulogy

The reality of leaving New Orleans:
All I did was move to higher ground
PTSD still presents itself whenever humidity
touches my skin

You will always miss the food but
not the racism. Miss the idea of home and not
the shell that remained once the water receded
miss the exaggeration of storms and a false
bravado of safety because

There will never again be a, "IF New Orleans
will flood" but "WHEN New Orleans will flood."
What will change next time?
once water returns to the sky leaving mold to
grow where human life use to exist.

exposing

a silt wasteland

a desert still inhabited by people that can't afford
to leave

inhabited by people

that have only known
of thirst

Socially distant

Refuse small talk. Unless its via text
Refuse time with family, unless it's a video call.
Refuse to touch my "essential" worker of a
partner
Just sit on opposite sides of the room with the
windows open. Kiss each other like you kiss your
grandparent. A peck and nothing else

This is the hardest experience for someone who's
principal love language is touch
To not feel a hug, a kiss
To be distant socially even if a person lives with
you just because society says they're essential

My veins constrict and vibrate uncontrollably
My goosebumps, a compass north arrow spinning
unable to find up
Signaling I'm lost within my own house
Lost while sitting on my own couch

My skin grows cold with the lonely of it all

No longer confident in who this body belongs to
Do it belong to the walls of my apartment that
I've been trapped in or vaccines or boosters?
Do it belong to my job who have reduced my
work since the pandemic or to my partner that
feels shame every time they touch me for fear of
making me ill.

When will my body be mines again
When will I learn to be social
With myself

Racism Casts a Spell on the Black Body
(Inspired by Sunni Patterson)

Doctors do this funny thing
When they speak to a black patient, they speak
to them in code

I told my doctor of a cough, chest pain and fever
He spoke in code. Said, "with your health history
of asthma and slight obesity lets wait a few days

to see if the symptoms persist "code for they
think I'm faking an illness, REFUSED TO
TREAT MY bronchitis for 15 days.

Medical aid withheld, even after I started to
cough up blood
They back tracked their records

Covered their malpractice by claiming
my delay in healthcare was due to a new covid-19
protocol, code for

Their Hippocratic oath only applies to white skin
with premium insurance
This Medical grade RACISM

The kind so potent
It looks like it's magical, just look at the spells,
The curse and HEX's it has cast on the black
body

looks like...pre-existing conditions
Cancer without any family history
Heart attack without any family history

Doctors will call this genetic predisposition
They will talk about how the black body shows
greater fat and muscle

No talk of the generations being forced to bread
to produce the biggest black buck
Doctors will talk about how the black body can't
control hormone or stress

No talk of the generations being forced to live
next to chemical plants because their white
neighbors lobbied to make sure their white
neighborhood is upwind from the polluted
byproduct

And since we can't call the poor health in the
black community
The evolution of racism
Can we at least call it

A blue cross and shield burning on our front
lawn. It's Black women 3 times more likely to die
during childbirth

Like telling your doctor you're in extreme pain
from an open wound and they only prescribed
aspirin

Because according to your insurance and your
melanin
Pain relief medication is not covered

This
medical racism with my blackness not covered

Leaves me guessing
That reduced life expectancy is the main
preexisting condition of blackness
When asked to rate this pain between one and 10

I would rate this generational curse
Off the charts
I wonder

if the fear of an early death causes genetic
depression, insomnia, and weakness of the heart
Or is this just a game show

Can't call it the new Tuskegee experiment
So, they will simple call this
survival of the fittest

Lets see how many black folk can endure major
medical surgeries without pain medication

Because black people lie about our
experience of pain

Just look how numb we must be to even
exist

My friend Nicole would say
That same numbness makes our skin age
slow
Nicole told her doctor of back pains
The doctor spoke in code and told them to
drink more water
Turns out. It was stage 4 kidney cancer

During her Chemo, a nurse will comment
about how young Nicole looked for her age
       Code for a beautiful corpse is the only
thing covered under your insurance premium
       At the funeral, her friends will gather
       And reminisce on
       Just look how beautiful and wrinkle free
the skin
       Of a beautiful black body
       That died a few months before,
       At the ripe old age of 32.

INTERSECTION
(after Kyla Janee Lacy code switch)

Black Boy caught between the crossroad of hate

One side: I'm a Nigga
One side: I'm a Faggot

When they intersect, they often look like Black
Queer boy burned alive by his mother in Jamaica
Black Queer Boy shot in his head by his father in
Nevada because he'd rather have a dead son as
opposed to a gay son
Black Queer Boy shot in his head in Rural
Louisiana because his white neighbors would
rather a dead nigga as opposed to a gay one
Often Look like Black Queer Boy Homeless after
coming out to his parents sleeping on the streets
of New Orleans
or Atlanta
or Washington DC
It looks black queer boy gets jumped at school
In New York
In Chicago
In Los Angeles
It looks like a death
In Rural Alabama
It looks like a lynching
In Tampa
The intersection of Black and queer look like
A black boy bashed until he meets God Early
But the details of his death will never be News
Worthy
Unless he Experiences a resurrection

Haiku 5 Through 15, Progressive Realization of Blackness

5.
to be a Black man
is to be a body bag
minus the toe tag

6.
to be a queer man
is to love in face of those
that want me to die

7.
to be from New Orleans
is to be seen as
slaves missing Angola

8.
ode: love being Black from the south
I must love pain
like a masochist

9.
to think racism will die
is to love like a masochist while chained

10.
evolved racism
unchained white aggression
all still based on Black hate

11.
times have changed

turns out to remember racism
makes you a racist

12.
turns out
that only applies to Black people before
shot by white men

13.
Black women can sleep
and be killed in life as she dreams
still no arrest

14.
my Blackness for sale
Kanye West the auctioneer
all a distraction

Excerpt from" The Meaning of the 4th of July For The Negro" by Fredrick Douglas. an Erasure.

What
              day that reveals   more
                              gross injustice and
cruelty
     , your celebration   a sham; your
liberty,   unholy   your nation

              empty and heartless; your
denunciation of tyrants
                                        a
hollow mockery;   your
sermons

              -- a thin veil to cover up crimes
                  a nation of savages .
                        guilty of practices
shocking and bloody

Go   roam
through

     every abuse
     , lay your facts by the side of the everyday
practices of this nation, and you will
                  revolt   shameless
            America

the dark

country.   forces
                        down   slavery.
                        t   o   the
doom of

Independence
      the   American
spirit

                              the same
old path of its fathers

established

            social
                        privilege
                        mental darkness
                              of
            cities
                        has borne
away   Intelligence
penetrating the   globe.

      on   Wind, steam, and lightning

      nations

            annihilated. —   expressed

on one side of the Atlantic   heard on
the other.

Emmett Recalls Life from Heaven

They used to call me bo bo

The nickname I earned because of the mistakes
I made in my youthful exuberance
Where I'm from, there's no such thing as white
picket fences-Doesn't matter what hood you're
from in Midtown Chicago Heat

We only know one thing. The sun
is beaming and the steam
Rising from the concrete
make this perfect weather for candy.

That I can crack jokes and mid cackle that
sounds like a wolf whistle. Here, black children
are free to laugh.
Without consequence.
Especially when the sunlight is glistening.
Summer was by far my favorite season.

That summer my mother sent me back
to her home in Money Mississippi. She hoped
that I would have fun with family and feel
the love between watermelon seeds and sycamore
trees.
But these Summers South below the Mason-
Dixon line was not made for short quick-witted
folks with smooth northern lips.
Thought that the only problems I would have to
worry about was mosquitoes that attacked
my face but it was
fist.

I should've listened when they told me to mind
my manners in Money. That their conversation
was not like honey.

No kind of melliferous
I never knew a whistle could be so serious.

Now my disfigured face is the image of the Civil
Rights Movement. The first Black body
to go viral without a hashtag.

My dead face
haunting America for generations.

Until they forget and repeat with Trayvon
Forget and repeat with Ayanna Jones
Forget and repeat with Tamir Rice

It's funny
As the Black child body count rises
You won't be able to rake over the mistakes of
this country without passing up my obituary.

My death will be common knowledge
But not how they would drag me down a shell
road
Head hitting deformations in the street leaving
small cracks in my skull- Split easily like a
watermelon
        They will not recall how pee leaked out of
        my bladder with every blow

They will recall that my head was affixed to a
cotton gin. Not that they identified my corpse by

the ring on my left hand because my face was
unrecognizable. A ring engraved with my father's
name "Louis"
A permanent fixture within my signature:
Emmett Louis Till.

Before the gunshot I thought
"where is my daddy?"
All I can think of is "I want my mommy"
She will be heartbroken without me

Instead, her son has become a ghost story.
A cautionary tale

Look what down south freedom will do to a Black
boy.
How they take the whiskers
of my soul and make violin strings
How they play an ungodly hymn
About my body being part of that song Miss
Billie sang

I just
never before seen strange fruit
That have fallen into the river
Without ever knowing how it feels
To hang from
A tree

Strange Contradictions

English is a strange language

There are words that are spelled the same, or sound the same but have two completely different meanings

Called HOMONYMS

I call it A contradiction

English is much like America

A land where your words can be miscued based on how they decide to define your existence

This country will have you stacked with a mountain of bills that are unbending. Making it hard to unbend stress into happiness

America would make you believe racism was **finished** in the 60's, the 70's just for it to resurrect and **finish** off George Floyd, Tamir rice, Rykeia Boyd within **minute**s

The **minutes** of all the court cases will spell acquittal for the racist fingers pulling the **trigger**

Their families are **triggered** just by seeing a white person with a fire arm

The fear will **garnish** the destruction with political correctness as those that protest get

their wages **garnished** for using their first
amendment rights.

The police chief will make **amendments** to his
statement once the police Cam footage become
public. Apologizing

The **public** will **refrain** from taking the police
report seriously, Thee outline is the same ole
refrain said every time someone **dies** on
"accident"

The blood will **dye** the street red with a life
snuffed out too soon

When people pass the crime scene, they sniff and
snuff at the stench of decayed

Remnants of a **tongue** saying "please don't shoot"

A mouth that will never pray in tongues on the
sabbath

The Devil is Present at the Protest

He's aware / that a great wrong has occurred /
that we are trying / to stop the wrong / he feasts /
on the resulting strife / the Devil / is at the
protest / but he can't show / his face / outright
ohhh noooooooooo / he must come / in disguise /
to blend in / dress in all Black / and a gas mask /
to infiltrate / or plain clothes / police / to
accidently throw a rock / and hide his hand /
to get mothers / fathers / there to protect / their
children /tear gassed / the devil / is in the tear
gas / so he arrives / covered / to the brim / but
through his mask / he can be seen / as the white
guy breaking / windows with a hammer / then
watches / the media / blame Black people / the
Devil / will encourage riots / transform / into a
white woman / setting fire / to Wendy's seen clear
/ as day / but media / will still blame Black
people / the Devil can look / like a flash grenade /
pepper spray / a rubber bullet shot / directly at a
Black teens face / the Devil's joy / will look
like that / teen's jaw / halved agape / down to his
chest / but the media / will blame the Black teen /
for being in front / of the bullet / will say / if he
would not have been / with these BLM protestors
/ destroying the country / he might still have a
face / won't say / he was unjustly attacked / by
police / because he spoke out / about unjust
attacks / from the police / the devil / is occupied /
at the protest / not protesting /he's selling t-
shirts / even though his views / are opposite / he
subverts / the message / by responding with
violence / he will have witnessed / time and time
again / that when you confront / peace with

violence / people switch / from wanting justice / to wanting revenge / quickly /if you're white / will turn from Martin Luther King/ to Malcom X / even quicker / the devil / came to the protest / and was shocked / that the protest was mostly white / so he was inactive / at first / cause he thought this protest / was about Black lives / the devil / believes that no one should think / of Black lives / even though everyone like to enjoy/ Black profit / just not the Black people / that died for it / like Black culture / but not the people / that died / just for making art / the devil / will most likely be there / in the middle / of the crowd / he might be / a rapist scoping / out his next victim / hiding / under the guise / of a Black man / destroying the women / that's march against / the destruction of Black men / the Devil / is busy / and he is too / preoccupied / causing confusion / separating / sowing doubt / to care / about justice!

My Blood Be – a prayer...

A slave ship, speech when English is forced on an
African spirit, its

                desserT Fo" Da Massess an' A
acquired Tastee If chuu DeCIDEEE ta luv It.
It will love you back. Heat up to match the flame
of your heartbeat. It will stay up all night to
become your best journal. rememberinn evree
detail O' YO'" smile in New Orleans EbonIcs
Black talk, AAVE[1]

Because of AAVE[1] some would say
my blood be not deserving of a good thing, look
how they lied
Now, white people use AAVE[1] in the news
it's funny how a television can become a slave
ship. A transatlantic rebellion of English now
gentrified!

The theft of my history and the constant
appropriation of culture lead some to
Needing a pill to prevent their life from becoming
toxic,
Some live life a blunt away from their blood
leaving the home of their veins; if only to find a
more loving environment than how society treats
black skin. A place with fruit and trees; clean air
and water. Top education and music and love
jammed into gardens. The zest of peace a
constant flavor in the collard greens.

Hopefully this thought of happiness is more than

1 AAVE = African American Vernacular English

24

a dream. Let it become a tree, with leaves that
have no problem surviving the desert. Give that
happiness purpose.

Give this blood back its importance, let it spill for
something righteous instead of decayed images of
its double helix. Let it kill itself and become new
without anyone even noticing.

My blood be
A silent phoenix. it be that magically gris gris,
that special ingredient
To conjure healing for broken hearts to beat like
they were never broken.

Let it be that heaven-sent resilience, that living
anyways in spite and in joy of blood.

My blood be
An afro pic
It's naps with roots like maps to my heritage
It be a cherry on top of a sundae or a pickled
okra, because my blood got range and fuck it, it's
complicated but its still good blood.

That sometimes stays up all night and
documents its own pulse in Ebonics. Black
talking about a smile that this blood finally
owns.

False Truce

The NFL decides to play
Lift Every Voice
before the national anthem.
Lift every pseudo-truce
and Black people
 are supposed to love
football again.
We are supposed
to be excited
about the prospect
of watching men
throw their bodies
 against each other
for entertainment.
Forgot Covid
is going to cancel
the football season
anyway. The NFL thinks
"Let's just announce it
so people can stop thinking
we're racist. We can't
get any Black people
to perform
for the Superbowl!!!!"

By the time they get to the second verse

they will conveniently forget
when Black players
tried to make a statement
so that Black people
would stop
being killed

unjustly, they were told,
"Shut the fuck up.
No thoughts
about lifting voices.
Work my field."
They told them
"No opinion nigga
boy. I own you,
all you know
is the field.
You think
because you can grow
your nappy ass hair
 out while still being
employed that you
can do anything?
Acting like you
didn't sign,
seal and deliver
your future
for TV ratings?
Work my field.
This is a sophisticated
type of sharecropping.
You make millions
and I make billions.
You have brain damage
and die before 60.
I bathe in the after birth
of infants so I will be
around until I'm at least 102.
This is your dream
that I made.
Come true boy.
Shut up.

Throw that ball.
Run,
like all good bucks."

Whack ASS Patriarchy

In August 2020 Cardi B and Megan Thee
Stallion
Released an ode to women enjoying sex and
praise for the WAP
The majestic and body rejuvenating
Wet Ass Pussy
Conservative Ben Shapiro
Response was that He
As a conservative...   white man
have never seen
such a thing
That his Wife's lady parts have never been wet in
his presence
That if the Pussy is Wet then it must be sick

And I think,
What A long way to state that you have never
pleased a Women
a long way to say that the only W.A.P. your wife
has experienced is your **W**hack **A**ss **P**atriarchy
That a woman has never fantasized about you,
even after she has had you
That she has tried to forget the dry rub, forget
your limp uncooked noodle
Thankfully, your money has fed her appetite.
Thankfully, she decided to cook and clean to get
her ring because the alternative was
heartbreaking

What a long way to say that you are so
unattractive
That the mere thought of you will make every
woman's vagina in a 50-mile radius clam shut

That you don't have a Mack truck of any size
And there's no garage that want to house you

I bet; your wife has never been satisfied
And I'm praying for her
It's evident
That you have no idea how a woman's body work
and you have two daughters
And I'm praying for them too

Dear lordt
(please bow your heads)
Please protect all women from men like him
He's a certified geek
7 days a week
He has no game
And his dick game weak huh

There's some Misogynoir in this house
        Misogynoir in this house
                Misogynoir in this house
                        Misogynoir in this house
There's some Misogynoir in this house
        Misogynoir in this house
                Misogynoir in this house
                        Misogynoir in this house
There's some Misogynoir in this house
        Misogynoir in this house
                Misogynoir in this house
                        Misogynoir in this house

Please protect these women from this
Whack ASS Penis
May they get their boots and their coats to
And flee from your

Whack ASS Penis
You went to college and paid a tuition just to
spread
Your Whack ASS penis
Man you a lame cause you believe
In your Whack ASS Penis

In the food chain, no one will eat ya
Your opinions are trash, a bottom feeder
Big D stand for biggest denominator in your
stupidity and your hypocrisy
Is you. You're strange
You asked who is it.
And wife was sleep and dreams don't have a
name

Now from the top, make it drop, that's whack
Patriarchy
Now get a bucket and a mop, that's some wet
Patriarchy
I'm talking WAP, WAP, WAP, that's some whack
ass Patriarchy
Macaroni in a pot, lactose intolerant-archy...huh

There's some Misogynoir in this house
        Misogynoir in this house
                Misogynoir in this house
                        Misogynoir in this house
There's some Misogynoir in this house
        Misogynoir in this house
                Misogynoir in this house
                        Misogynoir in this house
There's some Misogynoir in this house
        Misogynoir in this house
                Misogynoir in this house

Misogynoir in this house

Picked Up

When a couple approaches you for a threesome

Do not panic
Maintain your sexy, breathe
remember you're sexy
It's what brought them to you in the first place
Think about the service you will ...have been
providing
Think of the happy homes and dead sex lives
across the Gulf coast you will ...have resurrected

They will ...have remembered you as Nazareth
All you remember is how your insecurities
zombie apocalypse across their backs
The afterglow of afterlife will...has
Reminded you that this is your freak calling card
You do...have done this
 5 times without you even knowing

Without knowing that you we're... are just the
decorated freak of the evening
You've been...will be doing this all your adult life
Being sexy
Being used
Good to spice things up
That must mean your aura be Louisiana hot
sauce

An extra flavor for a meal
Never a full course

Elegy To My Hoe Phase

Here lies the phase of my life
where I was most sublimely
fucked
in every direction

Though the orgasms felt like the universe
exploding and creating life
the aftermath was messy
and emotional

I've never had this much tail before
and it showed
I gained a reputation of good dick
but not a good person
yet I gleam
with pride

I was freer with this body
after a clean bill of health
using the fact that I'm using
protection as an excuse
to enjoy flesh

I was hurting and thinking random
sex partners would fix it and no one bothered to
know, but I will be the first to tell you
I'm not a hoe

I'm was just very... friendly

I never dealt with life in excess
Though the fun that was had

to every part of my pelvis and mouth
was available and plenty
and wet
or hard
but delicious at all points in time

Here lay my morals
Couldn't bag a hot girl or guy
Slept alone most nights because he never made
the first move
His life meaning still hold value
but only in Christian abstinence circles
I remembered him often
but not often enough
to not increase my body count

Fun fact
body counts restarted
every time your body replaces
every cell down to the bone
So new body equals new body count
When that happens
do that mean that my hoe
phase is null and void?

Could I declare myself a born-again virgin?

Would I no longer have to repent
for all those times I've defiled this body
if that body is only a memory
that I no longer have time to remember?

Wonder If the Grim Reaper Has a Mother...

Did they escort her
to the other side

after she spent an eternity
giving birth to them?

Is she proud
of her child's life choices,

how they deals
in death and can't keep

Their perverted hands
to himself?

I wonder
when the grim reaper said

They were going to become
the gateway
to the afterlife,

did their mother ask
him to instead become

a tax attorney?
A guidance counselor?

Dentist?

Did she want her child
to be the source of smiles

instead of eye pupils dilated
without any reconstitution?

Does she think they be drug attic?

How they're addicted
to last breathes.

How they need
about 150 thousand hits

or they can't sleep at night.
Is his mother concerned

that they're always on the road?
Does she send them care packages

so that they don't get home sick?
You know they say hurt people

hurt people.
It's obvious the grim reaper

has some deep rooted
psychological issues.

Is that why they're not remorseful
that they were the only one working

during the pandemic?
They like to claim they're out

of work like the rest
of us; it's evident,

he's been busy.

It's evident,
that they have permanent employment

like the moon, the sky, the sun, the stars.
Don't they feel like they should take a day off?

Even the sun and moon have an eclipse.
Even the sky sleep on clouds sometimes.

Don't they think it's time
for them to relax

go to a beach for a minute and put their feet up
and drink a margarita?

Don't they think it's time
for them to take
a vacation?

The Ocean Drowns Things

My relationship with the ocean is tricky
My relationship to the ocean is,
"I don't know how to swim"
My relationship
with the ocean is I only know
how to survive when I'm not on its shores
Last time I lived beach side the ocean sent waves
that crushed me, asked me to come back
after it sent me inland
and me
Silly creature
that once crawled,
from her water, figures,
"If I come back humbly to her gulf
on peaceful terms
my soul won't
wash away."

At ocean's command
I returned to drown in her
waters in silence, forgetting the ocean
has never known peace. So therefore, her home
is never peaceful. There's so much anger
here, the calamity of waves
crashing causes so much
commotion, meaning
the sound
of my death
will go unnoticed
Meaning the ocean
has organized my death and I didn't
even know it until *years* later. Meaning
the ocean often *deals* in neglect but still seek

love that do not belong to her. There's reason
the ocean always has storms brewing. It's
the byproduct of her shame. There's
a reason her Tsunamis
are charging
constantly.
It's a byproduct
of her pride. She showed
me time again, she doesn't know
how to love. So, if you choose to love
the ocean, don't expect the ocean to ever love you
back. She's shown that love is not how
the ocean deals with things.

She's a sleeping tempest
sends hurricanes
to shores
just to remind you
that her diet has been polluted.
Calls you back from your shelter inland
to tend to this warm body death.
Then will, just as quickly,
play victim when I
don't remember
to care
about her
decay. Will become
still for once. When you begin
to treat her the way she treats you
Guess the ocean only called me to shore
to let it be known she was not going to die
without a fight. Guess the Ocean Wanted to
make sure I knew this murky bayou water is
where I crawled up from. Wanted me to
remember that this is the water

that made me. Held
a entire food chain
in her blood
just
so I can grow
comfortably. Remind me
that all its glory is beyond
my view. Remind me she has tried
to be damn near omnipotent, but is common
and imperfect most of the time. It can't think
rationally most of the time. doesn't know how to
communicate most the time, and don't give a
fuck to learn either. She just expects you
to erode in silence. Just want you to be
quiet as she treats you like trash.
Funny, that the ocean can't
handle when she gets
treated
like the trash
island she has
for a heart. Because
you realize that's what
she deserves. Because you
realize this particular ocean
can't change and it will always be
exactly what it is. Polluted.
Toxic. Call me
unappreciative
refusing
to drink
from
a well
that only loves
what it can control.
Refusing to tend to an ocean

that will curse your existence and
call it character building. An ocean that wants
a punching bag and not a son. The ocean
says she will never "be kind"
to the creations that came
from her volcanic
underbelly.
Not like when
strangers come to police
her shores. She's has to be nice
to strangers, she respects them. So I told
the ocean from now on, I'm a stranger,
and she won't have to worry
about me ever paying
a visit to dip
my feat
in her waters.
If I come, it'll be after
all her water has evaporated
into space. By that time
I would've gotten
over never giving
the ocean a
single wave
goodbye.

In the Name of My Creator, I Pray...

Heavenly mother on earth
Giver of all things
me
Made me believe in white god
But honestly everything I learned about him,
I see in you

So excuse me, for thinking
you be God,
mother,
I learned of your love

How Shepherds
or my siblings
would write commandments
about the rules in your house

Thou shalt not eat in your room
least you get roaches

Thou shalt not sleep if dirty dish is in kitchen
sink or mother will grab a belt and wake that ass
up!

Thou shalt not talk back
or thou shall get smacked

Thou shall only speak when spoken to
or you will get smacked

Thou eyes shall never roll
or they shall be snatched from socket

Thou shall keep no dirty clothes in bedroom

Thou shall not enter the front living room. We called it the president room. Only can go in if you're the president

Thou shall not have sex
under her roof

Thou shalt not let her know that
In the 12th grade that
you got your girlfriend pregnant...
under her roof

Thou son shall not bring home a man
talking about that's my boyfriend

Favorite Son

I was 17 when I told my mom I was bisexual

Her response
when she realized I broke
all of her commandments

> "when your male cousin
> raped you as a child
> you must've like it"

My mom once told me
I was her favorite son,

Being that she is God I guess she was upset she
thought a queer Black man Jesus

But on this day,
she saw me as Lucifer
at the gates of her heaven
Acted
as if her best friend's daughter
molesting me was a prayer answered
instead of my damnation

Acted
as if a 6-year-old boy
forced to lick a woman's privates
while on her period
was supposed to be
An Eden of manhood

As if,
my body

was a baptismal pool
meant to erase family sin
when they decided to bathe in it

The day I told my mom I was bi
she stopped eating the food that I cooked
The way homophobia works in New Orleans
Didn't want my queerness to leak
into the red beans or the gumbo

The day I told mom I was bi
she told me

"you needed the house of Jesus
you will catch AIDS and die
Don't embarrass this family
Never let anyone know
I'm going to take me you to a psychologist
to fix you or don't bother coming home"

Her house hasn't been my home since

They say a mother is the first god
a child ever knows,

If she is God
on that day

I became an atheist

Apathy

I was taught love—means I care so much for you
I would sacrifice
existence
just to make sure you're without harm

Some say the opposite of love is

                                    hate

I say the opposite is called
indifference

But the opposite is actually...silence

The opposite is

            the block feature on cell phones

I only have a few people blocked on my phone

                            My college loans
I'll pay them when I get the money

                            My rapist
My mother gave them my phone number
Why... that's between her and God.

And

                            My mother

Blocked her house phone, cell phone
 text messages

Blocked email
postal packages
Smoke signals
Blocked carrier pigeons
Blocked mental telepathy

I'm learning to love her how she has loved me
                                        With indifference

Like when she sent me to a rapist house
because she needed free babysitting

                                        Indifferent
Like her sense of protection
when I told her
My older cousin of 15 years violated me
from 7 until I was big enough to fight him of
                                        Indifferent

when I Detailed all the ways her "favorite
Nephew" bent me out of shape

                        As she insists, he not go to jail
            says that's no place for HER loved ones to be

                        She said that he's not worth the time,
                the embarrassment, that he's not worth
                                        breaking up the family.

            She says
            that I will have to just deal
            Deal with his existence
                                made sure he still
received

a thanksgiving dinner invite

She says
"We don't have the money
to make him pay for what he did"

I said I already paid!
with my scars,
my depression
my body
was already used as sacrifice
Then at that moment
my mother transforms my childhood rape into
kerosene
fuel for her to use as she gaslight

When she's pressed about her enabling
She turns up the flame

Says
She "had other things she had to worry about
at that time, she can't remember,"
"I won't understand
what she was dealing with"
Said with dismissive arrogance
With a kind of indifference
lodged inside her tone

When I asked why
she didn't believe
My older sibling
that told her he was a rapist because he raped
them

Her answer

...

My mother is blocked from calling my phone
I learned from watching her,
                silence is quite the opposite of love
                        No contact is best
            when the person's voice become poisonous

And as long as I answer my mother's call
I will be infected with this poison too

her voice will always sound like
adults setting up their children to get raped and
then sleeping well at night,

After my mother's last call attempt that went
straight to voice mail

My sister called me
Say's my mom can't understand why I can't just
forgive her
Doesn't understand
how I could keep someone
that gave birth to me

                                    blocked

My answer

                    ....

Frankenstein

A monster with no name
But a duplicate of its creator
A life with no purpose but to exist
Body jig sawed into a specimen.
Consisting of the perfect parts
To become beautiful

In a fit of insanity or genius
I attempted to Frankenstein my body into a life
without all my trauma

During childhood I removed my face
Replaced it with one that always smiled
My old one looked like a whispered prayer that
God didn't answer

Replaced my eyes with one-way mirrors
Clear of purpose
Empty of confidence
Replaced my tragedy with blissful ignorance
Now the only thing this new version of me would
consider
any ill of society would be sexism

A body made up of different humans can't
possibly see race under the eyes of the lord that
have forsaken my creation

I would replace my background story
My family will become the most loving entity I
know
It's not backwoods, Hicktown

I replaced my skin with the hide of a lion when I
was a teen
My entire existence had Rape victim track marks
tattooed in flesh
Especially along my privates and clavicle

My lower back
Home of
Permanent lash marks from my
father's "discipline"
Replaced with tiger stripes.
Can't be an endangered abused animal, if I'm
made up of every apex predator on the planet

Replace my arms with tungsten steel
Or make them out of purred granite
Or diamonds
Anything that needless won't have the audacity
to penetrate
Not for a booster, not for blood draws

I will replace my breathe with wind
 I hope it'll be able to chime a song of peace
Instead of happiness with a side of survival guilt
Sing a song of contentment and mean it
Instead of faking it until you make it

Replaced my skin tone with more brown skin
because it's perfect
Replace my hair with itself
Because my black hair is perfect

Change my personality
Make it less serious and more uplifting

For no other reason
So I can listen to the god speaking within me
when I speak to myself

I then will be
The perfect man to listen to in the times of
despair
Then I will be
Beautiful...

But when I look in the mirror
I still see nothing but
A broken man
Same scars on my face from where a mad
scientist created me

Don't know how I would ever deal
If life decided to deal me a different hand
Than this one
that leaves me
a broken monster looking for a god

Vessels

I am merely a vessel in which popcorn is
consumed
I am only a container of emotions in meat form
I am a ghost distributed and stretched in verse
and when I read my poems, I haunt myself
I got mommy issues
I got daddy issues
But yet have no issues being a father figure to
children
I am exactly the truth, when all lies have been
rung out
I am a lighthouse, needing something shiny to
direct my light
I remember a time of when
I was light
Until I grew tired of space
Now I am space, Black, Expansive, became bored
so I became a sunset, (too much ego) so
Then I became the satellite, (too modest)
Then I settled on becoming the moon
I eclipsed my self
I turned blood color in the shadow of the earth
Became rain, became cloud, fell from the heavens
Came back up from the ground as a rose
Everything else around me was concreate
Then I decided to become tree
Take back the land that was taken from me
Then I become the air clean
Then I become the atmosphere holding life in
balance looking out at
All galaxies
Remember a time
where a light moved within me

Death Sentence

People say time heals all things
So, I look at my scars
They look like...

My doctor told me
I had a Death in my veins
Asked me for the names
of all my sex partners.
Then sent me out the door

At that moment, I noticed
the person that I used to know
was dead
and as I became death
I notice how my skin
didn't sit on my bones

the way it use to.
My blood is not healthy
it's a Black hole
in liquid form
making me this
a handsome oblivion

Told a potential lover
They said my body won't heal,
it's undesirable
blamed a kiss from me
on why they caught the flu.

Everyone I told switched
from looking at me as if I was alive
to them thinking I will be dead

soon

When I was diagnosed
no one told me the side effect of HIV
was DEPRESSION
As death I became depression
not the same

Skin collapsed on bones-spirit
so unhealthy my hair fell out,
I became sick blood in a test tube
not healthy-just functional

I forgot to take my name off the blood donor's
list; so when I received my 3 month call to
donate, I had to inform them that this blood
is no longer healthy

That these organs
are now marked unusable after death.
That all light from this star
is just the remnants of what has died
and no one has taken the time to notice yet

Just a Black hole
Don't want to gift oblivion
because a lover decided
to go past the event horizon

Sometimes I feel like I've already died
like I'm living on the other side of that horizon
and depending on the events of the day,
I've either gone to heaven or hell

When I can't sleep it becomes a hell
one where my body welcomes pain
muscle aches, insomnia
one of the side effects of my medication
As pain,
I became constant

and consistent as the day
like my pill regiment
Then days turned to weeks turn
to months to 7 years undetectable
as my body returned to normal

and my hair grew back
and I learned to love my skin
I learned pain
is a side effect of growth
and what isn't growing is dead

I had to find the beauty in that

Found the beauty in my body
and how it has a funny way of healing
if you fast for three days, you'll create
new white blood cells
2/3s of your liver can be removed

and in a few months your body will regrow
that organ back to its original size
Every 10 years you have a brand-new set of
bones, new voice, new eyes

Meaning that this body will **heal** itself
All I have to do is give it enough time

As **healing** I confronted my depression
I took the skin that was collapsed
and put some muscles underneath
Took the blood that was sick
added medicine to heal

Stopped listening to people
that thought my diagnosis was a death sentence
and committed to enjoying what the day brings
Time won't heal all wounds
but it'll make you look at your scars

and rewrite them as growing pains

BLACK LOVE IS...

my mother getting over her homophobia and
inviting me and my husband to thanksgiving

It's me knowing that I can't go because I love
myself more than mementos of abuse

Is learning what it meant to black through
experience and still finding joy when it's told that
it doesn't belong to you

It's knowing that every right belongs to you

Black love is making the best out of a bad
situation

Black love

Is being in an environment where being black is
not a threat to society

We're just here creating jazz, just here creating
dance, just here being all together sexy mother
(shut your mouth)

Well I'm just talking about black love

A love the encompasses all hope for peace

Is feeling wanted even when you're being
difficult

Is loving someone pass there generational curses
that have ran rampant through your family tree

Is learning how to carve out joy while being born
in a horror story

Is turning scraps into delicacies

Black love is like a silk press with no heat
damage
It's a curl defined in defiance
It's movement, it's fastest human 100m it's
fastest marathon

Black love is the boom in the baseline of a Stevie
wonders song
A Whitney Houston song
A Beyonce song
Black love is the clever Witt in a Lil Wayne song

The passion of Tupac song

The story telling of a Biggie song

A creative explosion like an Outcast song

Black love is asking my son for an animal
cracker
Then he pretends to place it in my hand
Before the cracker lands in his mouth and me
Letting him slide

Black love is freedom
BLACK LOVE IS FREEDOM

The kind
That no one can ever take away.

A LETTER FOR MY PARTNERS....

TO READ IF I DO NOT RETURN FROM THE
GEORGE FLOYD PROTEST
If they kill me

They will say that I was big
And black
And they would be correct

They will say that I resisted arrest
I was told never let anyone take.my freedom
away,
So, they would be correct
I resisted

They will say I had drugs in my system
The drug in question would be weed
Indicia specific. Doesn't affect the brain
but soothe the body aches that come
with being black in America

So yes, I will most likely have drugs in my
system

It will also include Wellbutrin, Celexa,
citalopram
But saying the police killed a clinically depressed
man
doesn't make a catchy enough headline

They will say that I was a criminal
They will dig through my history and say I had
unpaid parking tickets so I had it coming

The I stole a stuffed animal at 15 and I can't be trusted
That I never stood for the national anthem
I admit it!!!!
That's when I conveniently took a bathroom break

They will fabricate a reason for why a gun was pointed to my face
Will say that I was under investigation for a drug ring
A possible suspect for a robbery, a murder, tax evasion
Anything to prove
I still had it coming
Will say that because I know 3 types of martial arts, that I'm inherently dangerous
Forget that I'm naturally a pacifist
looking for an alternative to feeling safe as a black man that didn't involve me carry a gun

They still will say I had a gun
When they really meant my skin
Will say that my melanin was alarming
That the mere sight of it in my epidermis
was threatening the safety of society
That's why I had to be exterminated

So, PROTEST
And don't listen to any family members saying they forgive the people that murdered me...
They were probably paid off

IF MY KILLERS ARE ACQUITTED
RIOT

It's said, a Riot is the voice of the unheard
And since I'm dead with my murders running
free because they were just following their 6
months of police training
Riot

Burn down everything this country holds dear
Riot for Tear gas
Rubber bullets
Gestapo level kidnapping

Riot
Burn this country for Malcolm, Fred Hampton
and any leader of the African American
community that was killed
Simply because they were black

Riot for the revised history we learned
Cause no one knows MLK was Assassinated for
saying he was about to march on Washington
because America owed every black person a
check

Riot
Burn
Flip a car
Behead a statute

And this still will be more peaceful than
Shooting a black kid with a toy gun within 2
seconds of your arrival
More peaceful than kneeling on a neck until their
life slip away

If they kill me, you better make America
remember my name
Let it haunt them like an image of emit till
Let this country never be able to say
the pledge of allegiance without them first seeing
my blood on their hands

In one nation
That pray to the god of money only
And where liberty
Is a dark humor joke
And where there's justice

For some

Concrete Stomach
(inspired by ghetto twinz)

When a bullet explodes from a pistol, the hand
moves back as the bullet goes forward.

When the bullets hits skin, the skin
runs from entry and the bullet stops.

When the body drops, the earth screams
"Mmmmm, another one."

When a mother cries
over a dead child's body, a siren screams louder.

She ask, W.W.J.D. Then the family's heartache
somehow bellowed a grief church hymn

sung even louder. Mother now a hollow, body
confounded, that her womb still remembers

his imprint from month one. Then his sisters
weep, then his friends soon forget

and moved forward. But a mother,
her grief ceases-never, it's a bruise

with the throb of torn tissue that won't stop.
So she figure out a way to make it stop.

Thought the murder of her child's killer
could make her days move forward.

She wanted to know if she could make
his mother's octave cry of "Lord no"

a pitch louder. Her thoughts dimmed
from savagery to a mimicry of human

when she realized (1) She's doesn't want
to take a mother's child, especial her only one.

(2) she remembered even God watched
the Crucifixion of his only son,

so she screamed louder. Moved her bullet
to retreat from her pistol, it went forward.

The scream of the air says "redemption"
as bullet enters, flesh folds back,

then the heart beat stops. The body drops,
and the earth rubs it's belly,

saying "Mmmmm. I got another one."

"Call tha cops, forget tha cops,
won't ya grab tha glock.
No time to explain, my baby's been shot
With a AK, killa no way
Cuz I don't play, behind my baby
Lord...,
I heard my baby screaming
"mama come and squeeze me"
As I break down screaming "don't ya leave me"-
Momma's Hurting- Ghetto Twinz

On realizing I am black
inspired by Mwende FreeQuency Katwiwa

I found out I was a different race than other
people when I went to pre school

There are certain things you learn once
colonization befuddles your skin

Depending on how much sunlight it retains
It could feel like a black hole

Like, all life close, gets lost
Never to be seen again

Like when things go missing
Fingers fall into you
When you make a mistake
Fist disappears into your skin
And parents only see this as bruise
As he's troubled
Cause all things darker are trouble
Are harvest

Gather up before me
And watch wear everything that is light
Disappears
If you look at me long enough
I will look back at you
I looked too long
Got put in timeout for not paying attention

Got punished for walking out of line
Guess something in me knew this was a pipeline

I saw their tactics
Once the other "children" realized I was black
They saw me as scapegoat

A game
Let's get akeem in trouble by pushing
Then when he pushes back, it's an issue
I guess it was a prophecy for the future
When blue kill black
But if black protest blue it's an issue
Even though the reaction ain't quite eye for an
eye enough

Once I realized that everything and everyone, I
love was black
I became terrified
The spook almost turned me pale
Passable enough to survive invisible

There is no war...In Ba Sing Se

Welcome avatar, I'm Joo Lee
I will be your guide
for everything while you are here.
But before we get started

on the tour, I have to inform you
of one tiny thing so that you don't get in trouble.
You have to remember
that "there is no virus in Ba Sing Se."

There is no need to wear a mask here
there's no Corona virus.
Our leader says he will send all our children
to school regardless of this outside fear

from the Fire Nation. We are safe here.
No fire virus built against this stolen kingdom
shall prosper. So go to work,
go to bars, go to concerts,

don't worry, you won't be going
to a morgue, crematorium, graveyard,
not unless you're there to visit
the dead. Well, the old dead,

because no one dies
here, even though we have everlasting
gun rights, because no one...important dies
here, because there is no war

in Ba Sing Se. There's no one sick
here, what you see on TV is fake news.
The nurses are being big babies.

Soon they will have 'a change of attitude.'

Just like the protestors
in the northwest quadrant,
that might or might not have been kidnapped
by the Dai Li. I can neither confirm nor deny

if they have been converted
to no longer be violent,
to no longer have an opinion.
They too believe

that Ba Sing Se is "the best
place in the world."
Here, you can pull yourself up
by your boot straps, become anything

you want, as long as you were born
an Earth Bender and born in high class.
Must have both. Just having one
means you cannot partake

in the great USA–I mean–Ba Sing Se dream.
We have to make the Earth Kingdom great again
by being the shining example on the planet.
There's no covid in Ba Sing Se

Because we have the best test ever.
It can't get here from another nation.
Look at our southern walls.
Ba Sing Se boast the best walls,

the greatest walls. There's never been
a sturdier wall. What's that?
Why are the citizens so scared of us?

Because we need law and order

on our streets. The Dai Li is set to protect
our cultural artifacts. They will do so peacefully
because, you know, there's no corruption
in Ba Sing Se. But who will protect you

come November? I think we shouldn't
hold an election next year. You know, for safety,
at least until we get enough
hydroxychloroquine. It's a life saver.

Why am I taking it if there's no virus?
Just a precaution. When our leader
was sick, he was on a different regimen
of medicine. What medicine?

That does not matter. For everyone,
just take Hydroxychloroquine.
What do I have to say about the Dai Li
placing their boulder of a knee on a non bender's

neck for almost 10 minutes?
I think we need to wait
until we get all the information. The Dai Li,
they're just doing their job. They have a hard job,

an important job. Green Gestapo lives
matter. Make that slogan, into a poster
celebrating the peace and splendor
in our great nation.

On it, make sure you have a picture of a man
lying in bed with bleach going into his veins.

Love Language

Someone once loved me in a way I didn't
recognize
Loved me in the way that THEY saw fit

This is us

Not loving each other in a language that we both
speak

They tried to love me
By not communicating
Not calling back, by them being ok with me being
an afterthought
Their love tends to
Appear and function off of telepathy when I'm
not exactly a telepath
I need to hear you verbalize your thoughts.
I need you to make your "love" a verb backed by
your thoughts.
I need to talk to the person driving your space
ship, not the representative
I need honesty
If I'm wrong, I need you to tell me
If I'm right I need you to tell me. If I look
particularly handsome today, I need you to tell
me
If I need a shower, I need you to tell me

When people love me
in silence,
it feels the same as if they never loved me at all

A Gorgon's Hiss

I've been known to turn hearts to stone

Been known to be the last thing a person sees
before the other side greets them with granite,

      With concrete

        With limestone

Please,
Don't look at me too long...
I wouldn't want all this trauma to kill you
I'm socially distant for a reason

I'll turn your heart into a stone sculpture I'll
place in my garden for... no reason

Transmute you
      to whatever I need to complete my human
      demise collection

Your statuesque death will go perfect in my
garden next to my family tree

The tree in question
is...Rotting
      The insides,
      are filled with snake-like gorgons like me.

Expelled from the temple of our goddess-mother's
and left in the wild

Lost to wind

Just because we dare speak on how this family have defiled
The youngest of children,

The penalty when you bring a God shame?

Our names,
rewritten

Cursed as snake with snakes for brains

Instead of laying hands, all I can do is lay eyes

The hiss of my tongue and the glare of the reptiles growing from my head spells the end for whoever dare look at the monster my family have made of me

A family that would rather me be an outcast.
Unhealed and roaming about
Destroying unknowingly

Looked at as the lowest of the low
Instead of a creature you need to watch your steps around

Rather me be seen as trickster
Telling stories that convince some to partake in fruit

Would rather me be known as Slytherin, Then being seen as stronger than what Olympians have put me through

Excuse me

Please.

Excuse my cold bloody nature
It's the reptilian in my veins

It came with the territory
Thrust under my belly I'm forced to now crawl on
Please.

Be careful
Of the venom that drips from what use to be my
hair follicles
Even

The Olympians that cursed my existence
Know not to let me lay eyes on them again

I have no problem suspending the animation of a
family member
Who once tried to silence the hiss of my legend
Cast them in sandstone, something to erode
when it rains
Cast them as enabler
The starch defenders of a family's right to rape
and have silent victims

I have no problem seeing the
Contortions their body make in the most
uncomfortable pose of surrender

Freeze them in their complacency
Face a bust
casted in a torment
lasting forever

Destruction will look so perfect next to my
hydrangeas

ABOUT THE AUTHOR

Akeem Olaj is a Poet, Actor, Playwright, Architect,
Martial Artist and Activist born and raised in, New
Orleans, Louisiana now based in Austin, TX. He was
the Co-founder and coach of Slam New Orleans Poetry
Slam Team. As a Poet and Coach with Slam New
Orleans , affectionately nicknamed Team SNO, he's
achieved 3 National Poetry Slam championships (
2010 Group, 2012-13 Team) And 4 regional Titles(The
2016 -17 Southwestern Regional Champion,2017
Redstick regional champion , 2016 Southern Fried
poetry slam champion). With Slam New Orleans He
has also opened for Shriver's Row, Amanda Seals,
Kendrick Lamar and P Diddy and the family.

Individually, Akeem was featured in Russell Simmons
presents All Def Poetry Media in 2015 and 2016. He
has also opened for Big Freida, Alfred Banks, Ledsis,
Tank and the Bangas and Adia Victoria. He wrote and
starred in a one man play centered on The Louisiana

Reconstruction period for the National Reconstruction conference held in New Orleans in 2014.
He also is the Austin Poetry Slam Grand Slam Champion 2019 and a member of the Austin poetry Slam team 2019. The 2019 Individual of the World Poetry Slam Champion and the 2021 JustLissen Queer Slam Champion. He's a 3-time New Orleans Grand Slam Winner. And in 2014 Akeem was listed as the one of the top 40 people under 40 to know in New Orleans.

He Has performed at The Essence Fest, the New Orleans Fringe Fest, New Orleans Jazz Festival, At the New Orleans Arena with the Pelicans, Get lit Festival-LA, and 40 colleges including Harvard, Tulane, LSU, UNO, Texas AM, TSU, BERKLEY School of Music, etc. As a speaker/activist Akeem's has spoken at many conferences across the United States on topics ranging from domestic violence, HIV awareness, LGBTQ Rights, Louisiana Reconstruction time period, and Southern Art.

Made in the USA
Columbia, SC
23 May 2024

35648869R00050